Great Explorations

Contents

Written by Pam Rushby

Introduction

In the past, most people did not travel far. Any place that was more than a few days from their homes was a mystery. People thought that monsters and dragons attacked travellers. They believed stories they had heard about islands with strange peoples. People even believed Earth was flat. They were certain that if they sailed too far they would fall right off the edge of the world.

However, some people in the past did travel. They visited faraway places. They walked or rode horses. They sailed ships across the sea. They were explorers.

There were many reasons why people went exploring. Some went to trade goods. Some looked for new lands to live in. Some thought they could find gold. Some wanted to become famous. Others just wanted to see what was there.

Some people believed that strange people with just one enormous foot lived in faraway lands.

Some people explored new lands in the hope of finding gold.

Ancient Egyptian Explorers

The ancient Egyptians were explorers. They traded with people around the Mediterranean Sea and the Red Sea. They sold goods to other places. Goods like these are called **exports**. Grain and papyrus, an early form of paper, were the main exports. The ancient Egyptians also brought in goods from other places. Goods like these are called **imports**.

Ancient Egyptians used imported gold and precious stones to make jewellery.

Punt was one of the places the Egyptians traded with. It had things that did not exist in Egypt. People thought it was a faraway land full of mystery.

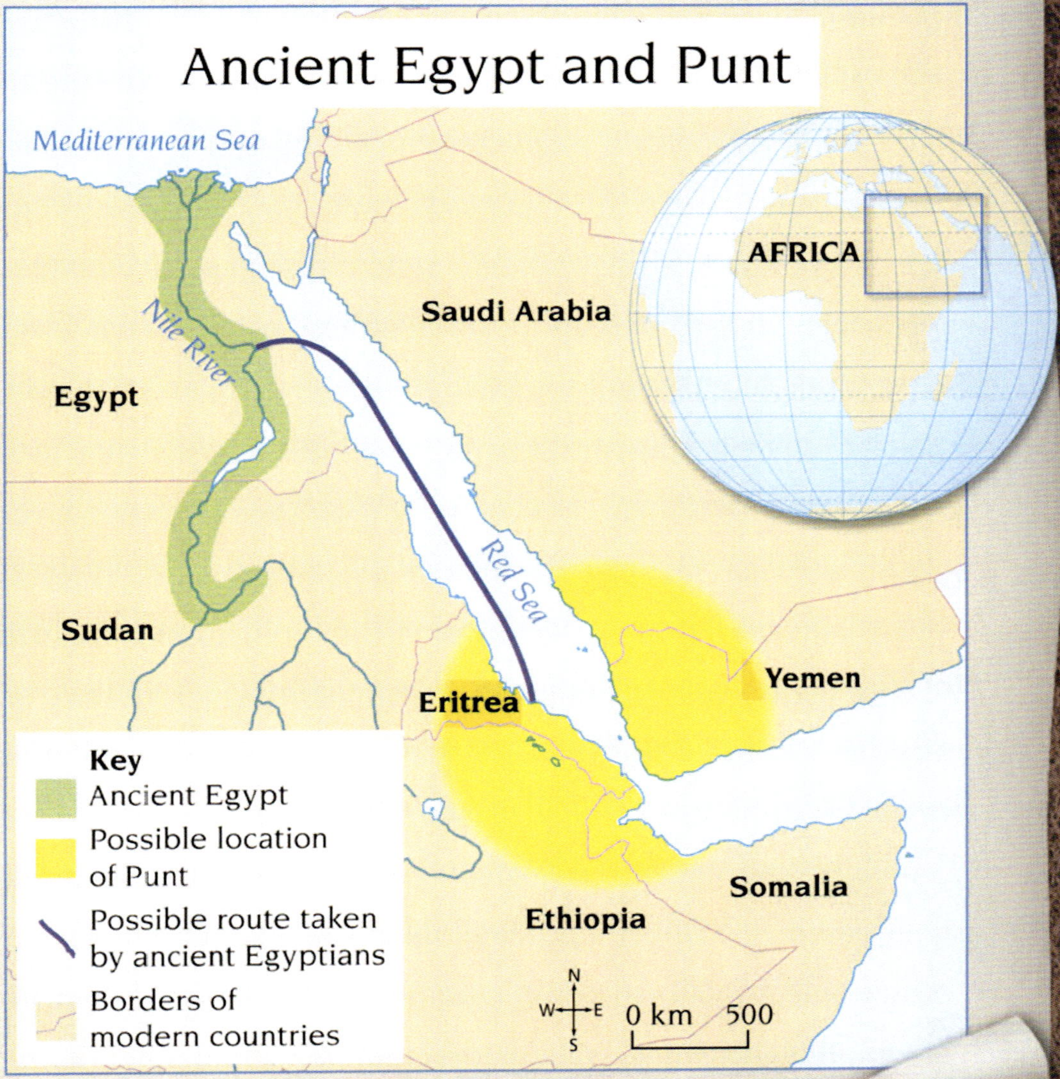

About 3,500 years ago, the pharaoh Hatshepsut sent five ships to Punt. She ordered them to bring back imports such as a fragrant gum made of hardened tree sap, called myrrh. The Egyptians used myrrh to make perfumes. They also burned it in their temples as incense.

The journey was very risky. Many people were sure the ships would never come back. However, the pharaoh was proven right. The ships reached Punt. They returned loaded with gold, myrrh, and special woods.

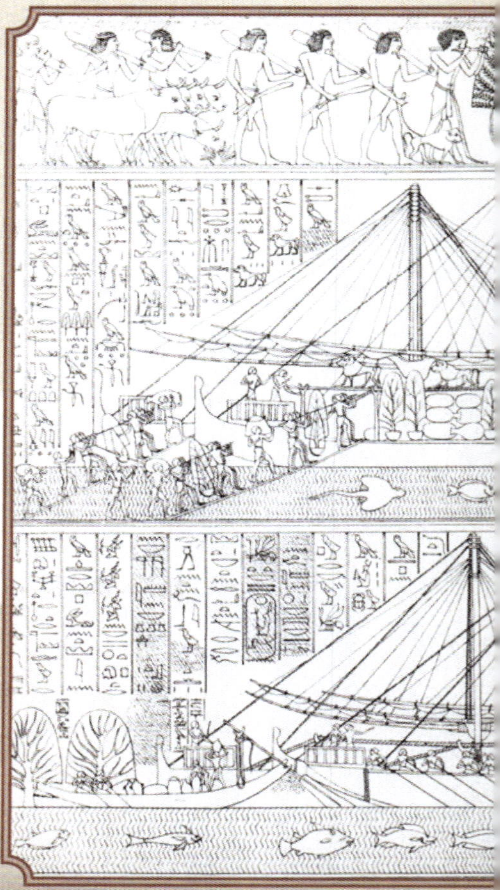

A picture from Hatshepsut's tomb showing her ships returning to Egypt with goods from Punt

A piece of myrrh, popular in ancient Egypt because of its pleasant smell

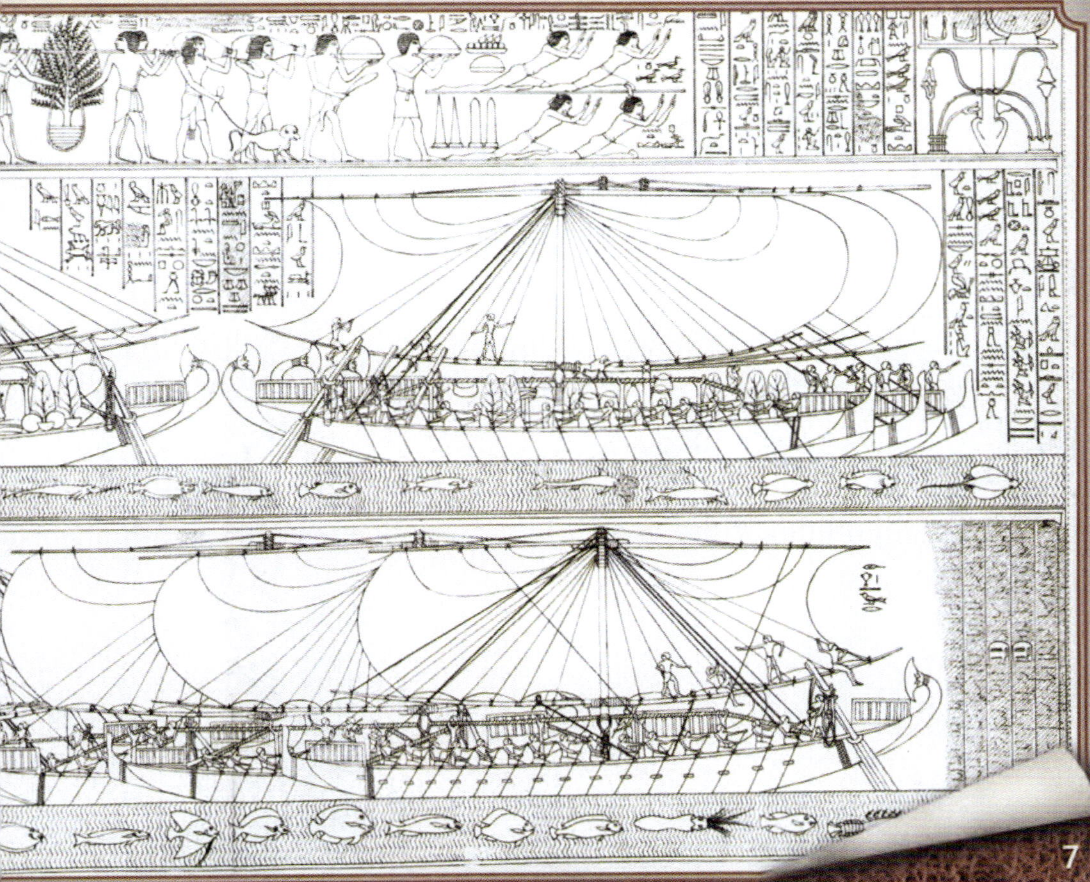

The Vikings

Hundreds of years ago, the Viking people lived in the north of Europe. People think life was hard there. There probably was not enough land that was good for growing food, or **arable land**. So, the Vikings went to other places to find what they needed.

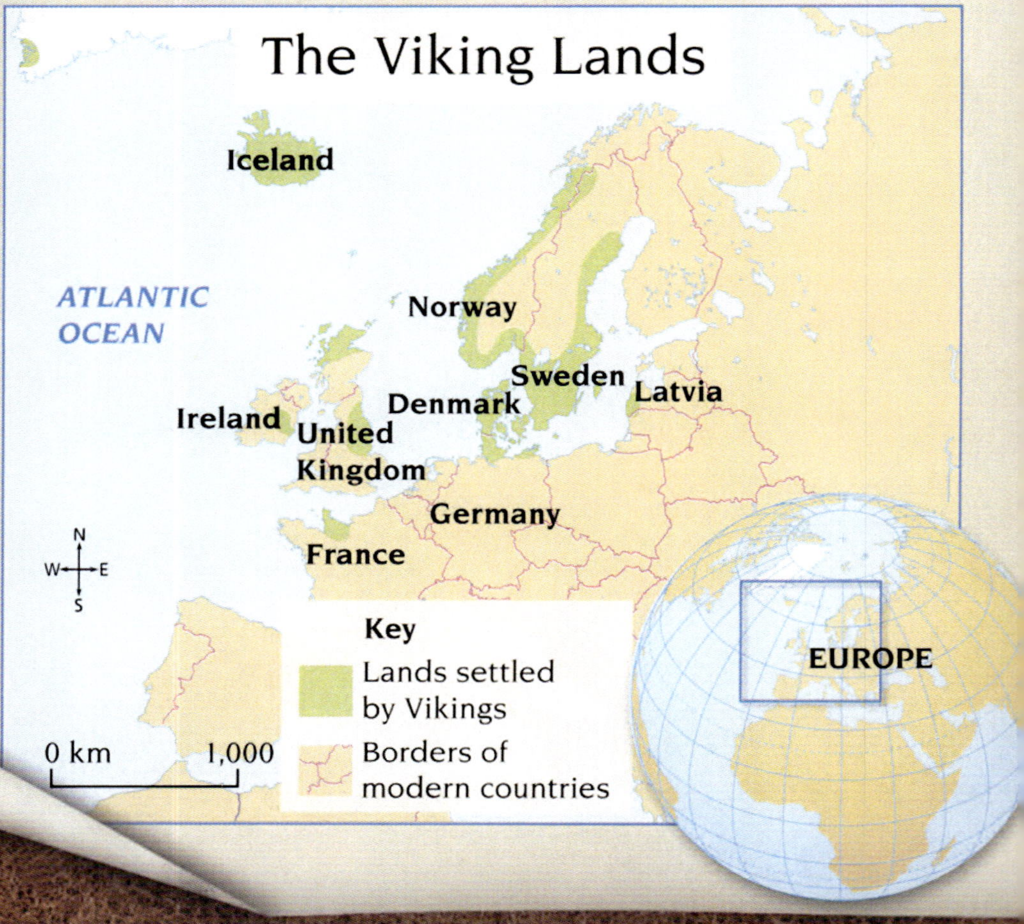

The Vikings were great sailors. In longships, they sailed off to find food or goods. Sometimes, they found new land to settle. Sometimes, they traded with other people. Other times, the Vikings just attacked other people. They stole their food, goods, and land.

A modern copy of a Viking longship

About 1,000 years ago, there was a Viking called Leif Erikson. He heard stories about a wonderful new land across the ocean. Viking sailors said it had mountains and forests. They believed it had plenty of good land.

Viking warriors were able to cross the oceans to find new lands because of their skill as sailors.

Leif Erikson sailed off to see if they were right. He probably sailed north-west first. Then, he turned south. He found a land with mountains, forests, and arable farmland. Today, people think this was Newfoundland. It is an island next to the east coast of Canada.

The Polynesians

The Polynesian people also explored to find new land. The Pacific islands they lived on were small. They did not have a lot of arable land. Some islands became crowded with people. Many people wanted to find new islands. They thought life would be better there.

The Polynesians explored the great Pacific Ocean in boats like this one.

The Polynesians knew a lot about finding their way from one place to another by boat, or **navigation**. They watched the sea, the sun, and the stars. They watched out for floating plants. These would tell them where land lay. They would look at the size and shape of the clouds and waves. They knew the birds that lived on and near land. They would watch the birds. Then, they could guess where a new island might be. Today, people think these journeys in the Pacific were amazing.

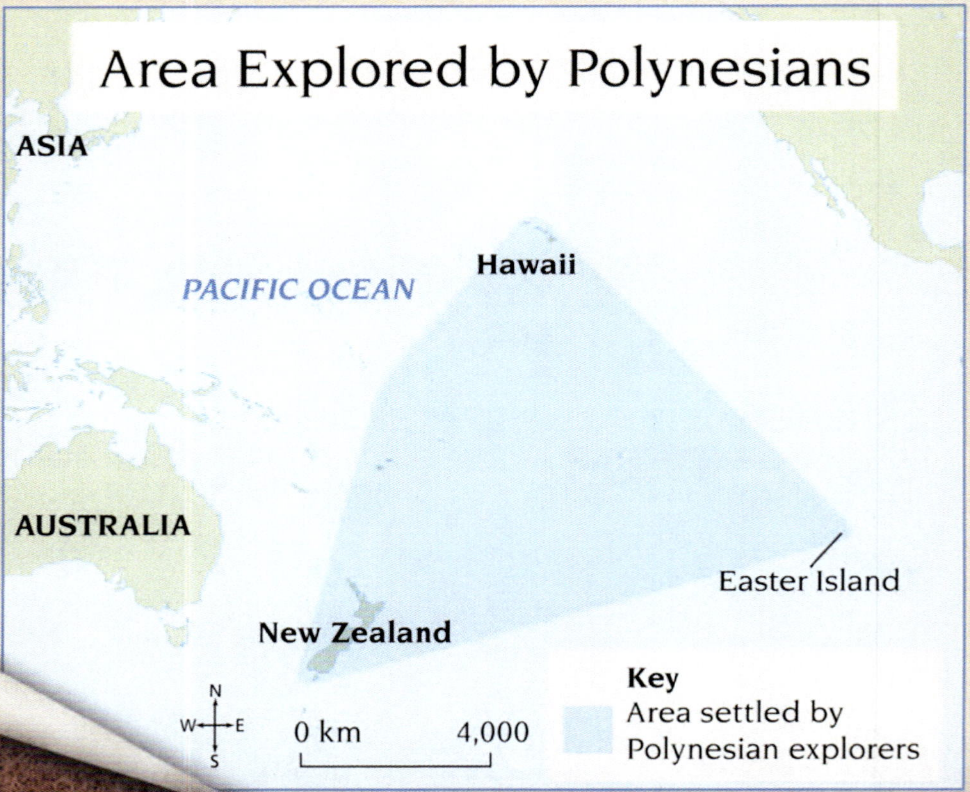

The Polynesians navigated with stick charts such as this one, which shows wave patterns and islands.

European Explorers

About 300 years ago, some parts of the Pacific were still unknown to people in Europe. They did not know about Australia and New Zealand. However, they believed there was a big landmass, or **continent**, in the South Pacific.

This map from 1595 shows *Terra Australis*, or *The Southern Land*, a large continent that people believed lay in the South Pacific.

Then, some European sailors saw islands off Australia's west coast. They said the land was wild and dry. They were sure there were strange animals. So, everyone thought the rest of the land was like that. However, they could not see how big the land was. They did not know they had found the southern continent.

The rugged coastline of Australia's west coast

In 1768, the explorer James Cook set out to find the southern continent. There were scientists and artists on Cook's ship. They were there to collect plants. They were there to draw the people, plants, and animals they found.

Captain Cook's first voyage took three years.

James Cook and his crew were good at navigation. Dutch explorers found New Zealand first, but Cook's crew were the first Europeans to sail around it. They were the first to see the east coast of Australia. They found that not all of Australia was wild and dry. They thought it was a good place to live. The scientists collected plants. The artists drew pictures. James Cook drew maps of New Zealand and Australia. People can still see these maps today.

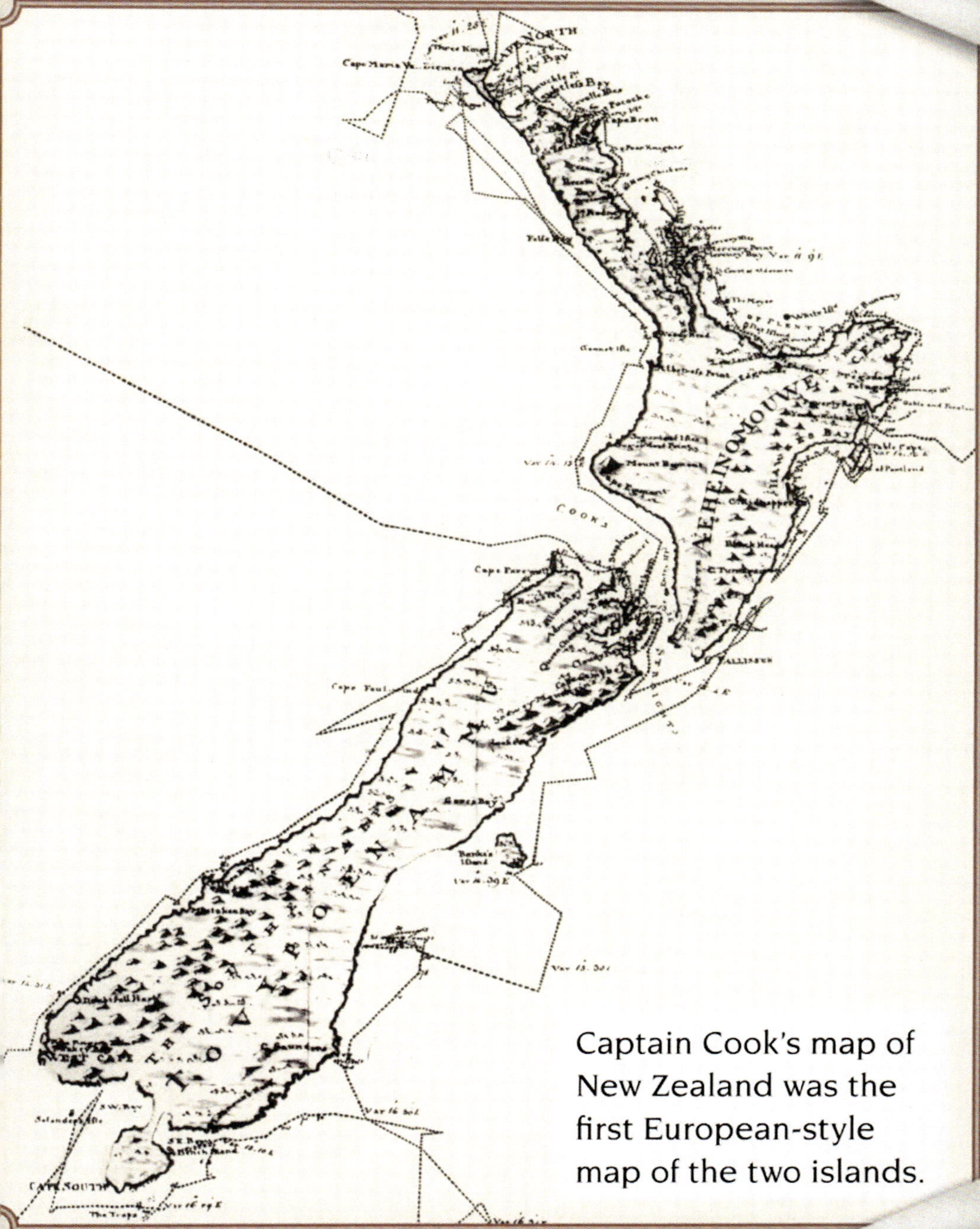

Captain Cook's map of New Zealand was the first European-style map of the two islands.

Space Exploration

In the 1950s, people started exploring space. First, scientists tested space flight with animals such as dogs. They sent dogs into space. Some dogs came back safely. So, when the first man went into space, people thought he would be safe. However, many other dogs died, so they could not be sure.

Laika was the first animal to orbit Earth

In 1961, Soviet cosmonaut Yuri Gagarin blasted off from Earth. Some people believed he would be crushed when his spaceship took off. They thought the spaceship would never come back. However, it took off safely. It orbited Earth once. Then, Gagarin came safely back to Earth.

Yuri Gagarin on board the spaceship *Vostok 1*

People will keep exploring space. There are billions of stars. There are very large groups of stars, called **galaxies**. Scientists have found black holes and dying suns. Many people believe there are new planets that humans could live on. Some people think there might even be new kinds of life in distant galaxies. Others say there is no life anywhere else. Scientists will explore further and further into space. They will find out who is right.

An artist's impression of future spaceships visiting a distant planet

Glossary

arable land – land that is good for producing crops

continent – a great landmass

exports – goods that are sent to other countries

galaxies – large clusters of stars

imports – goods that are brought in from other countries

navigation – finding and keeping a course from one place to another by boat or ship

Index